Simple as PQRST And U

YOUR RECIPE FOR ADDING VALUE BY MAKING DECISIONS AND TAKING ACTION

Randal Wells

Foreword by Emeritus Professor Gary Martin

PQRST And U www.pqrstandu.com

First published in 2020
PQRST And U
Australia
www.pqrstandu.com

Copyright © 2020 by Randal Wells

All rights reserved. Except for short extracts for the purpose of review, no part of this book may be reproduced, stored in a retrieval system or transmitted in any form or by any means, whether electronic, mechanical, photocopying, recording or otherwise, without the prior written permission from the author.

A catalogue record for this book is available from the National Library of Australia

Title: Simple as PQRST And U: Your recipe for adding value by making decisions and taking action

Print (paperback) ISBN: 978-0-6489956-0-9
Ebook ISBN: 978-0-6489956-1-6

Simple as PQRST And U is dedicated to:
My Dad
Until we meet again may God hold you in the palm of His Hand

Foreword

From the very first time I had the pleasure of meeting the author, Randal Wells, I got the distinct impression that his mind was literally overflowing with hundreds of untapped thoughts and ideas on how we as leaders, managers and supervisors might inspire better workplaces.

Now, we can devour those ideas in this cleverly written book and one that will satisfy even the most ferocious of appetites for self-improvement.

Randal Wells, tells us that invariably, we make the whole process of making decisions and taking action in our workplaces far too complicated.

He shares his view that we *scavenge on the carcass of complexity* - a powerful thought and one that prompted him to write **Simple as PQRST And U**.

This book will spark the imagination of anyone who's been at the heart of making important decisions with and for others.

The reader will be compelled to rethink what they know about leading others, through the use of a powerful analogy aligned with a very familiar and regularly performed task: following a recipe.

Randal explains that, like any recipe, there are some essential ingredients when it comes to working with others. At the same time, he makes the point that just like a chef, every manager or leader will need to tailor a particular recipe to the specific preferences of those who will be dining. In other words, he urges the reader to add in their own special ingredients to cater for the tastes of those working alongside the reader, and to reflect the special culture of the reader's work context.

Neatly dissected into four parts, the book is easily digested.

The first two parts systematically address each letter of easily recalled *PQRST*. These are what the author describes as the recommended ingredients for clarifying and getting fit for purpose.

The third part, *And U*, explains how the ingredients combine and how the reader can add their own personal touch, just as a good chef does.

The final part highlights a range of important considerations, or "food for thought", as the reader goes about following a recipe - or as leaders do - make decisions, take action and add value.

There's literally a buffet of important points of learning to feast on, including my favourite: that decision making processes might start with you, but they are not all about you.

Simple as PQRST And U provides the reader with plenty to "dine on" in helping them to become the chef and not simply the cook when working with others towards fulfilling purpose from an organization, team and individual perspective.

Emeritus Professor Gary Martin
Chief Executive Officer
Australian Institute of Management WA
Perth, Western Australia

Contents

Dedication   iii
Foreword   iv

Introduction   1

PART 1: Clarity of Purpose (P, Q)   7

P is for Purpose   10
Q is for the Question   12
Part 1 Takeaways   18

PART 2: Fit for Purpose (R, S, T)   21

R is for...   23
S is for...   33
T is for...   44
Part 2 Takeaways   55

PART 3: And U — 59

The Power of And	61
Treble U	63
It starts with U	65
It's not all about U	68
Blind U	72
Part 3 Takeaways	81

PART 4: The recipe in action — 85

Be the chef	87
Simply sweet	90
The test of the recipe	92
Next...	96
Master Chefs	97
My Unique Ingredients	99
Notes On Quotes	100
About The Author	114

SIMPLE AS PQRST
AND U

Introduction

Simple as PQRST And U is about decision making and action taking. Why? Because **your** value is the sum of the decisions **you** make and the actions **you** take. Simple as!

You may be a company director, or a business executive. You may be a company owner, or you may be thinking about setting up your first company. You may be a parent making decisions about your child's future. You may be a student studying towards your first qualification or your doctorate. You may have learned what you know through the school of life. You may have a specific decision to make. You may be wishing to improve the decision-making of your board or your team.

Whatever your reason for reading this book I hope you discover, or possibly rediscover, the simple ingredients to developing value for you, your family, your team, and your organization. This book is for you. It's your recipe.

There is no shortage of material on the art and science of decision-making and leadership. In fact, the volume of material is the overwhelming problem! And, with time constraints, how does one find, let alone remember, what you need to know? This book seeks to address the volume problem and help you recall what you need to know about making decisions and taking action.

I decided on the name of this book while listening to Tom Peters presenting *The Excellence Dividend*. During his presentation he reminded me of "a bias for action" from *In Search of Excellence*. I first wrote down Easy as PQRST And U. Tom then spoke about how the softer things are harder to do than the hard things. "Soft is Hard" he says. I realised PQRST and U is not necessarily easy. But it is simple. ***Simple as PQRST And U.***

My maternal grandfather, Dr EG Malherbe, held a Ph.D. and was awarded ten honorary doctorates from universities around the world. He was a great educator and had the knack of explaining things in a way that was simple and easy to understand. As a child I recall him saying, "If a person can't explain something to you in a simple way, he either doesn't know enough about what he's talking about or he's trying to mislead you. Or both!"

Making things appear complex is easy and it makes the problem to be solved appear bigger than it really is. To a significant extent many scavenge on the carcass of complexity. They are not motivated to make things simple. It takes effort, but it is worth the effort, to strive for elegant simplicity.

> *"It's easy to take something simple and make it complex: politicians and lawyers seem to do it for a living. Yet very few innovations are championed for their intricacy. Most are known for bringing elegance and simplicity to even the thorniest problems."*
>
> Larry Keeley

So as not to single out politicians and lawyers, I would add most consultants and many others to the list of complexity makers. My hope in writing **Simple as PQRST And U** is that I be omitted from the list of complexity creators! And that many others join me.

I anticipate that many of the ideas and concepts in **Simple as PQRST And U** will be familiar to you. If you find **Simple as PQRST and U** to be innovative, I hope it is for elegant simplicity and how existing ideas and concepts are packaged in a new way.

Master Chefs, the bibliography to **Simple as PQRST And U**, recognises the people whose ideas and concepts I have found valuable. Other ideas and concepts come from conventional wisdom. Some are my views, but those probably come from my subliminal learnings from others.

While writing this book I shared the concepts and framework of **Simple as PQRST And U** with many people including family, friends, clients, colleagues from the Australian Institute of Management WA (AIM WA) and Leadership WA, my barber, and strangers. In fact, anyone who showed an interest!

Through this process the concepts and framework have, I feel, been robustly validated by a diverse range of people in the real world. You may recognise your contribution to *Simple as PQRST And U*.

Simple as PQRST And U is a short book. Deliberately so.

Simple as PQRST And U is an easy read. I have tried to avoid words used by self-indulgent academics and in corporate speak. Simplicity is the key to clear communication. I have avoided using code language that only those "in the know" know. And I have avoided using acronyms. With the exception of PQRST And U!

When reading *Simple as PQRST And U*, keep in mind the words "you" and "your" apply in the singular to you, as an individual, but also in the plural to your team (or teams) and your organization. There are three levels of You. U and U and U. And also keep in mind it starts with you, but it's not all about you.

Think of *Simple as PQRST And U* as a recipe with recommended ingredients. Like all recipes, the result depends on the right quantity and quality of the ingredients. And personal touch. Each ingredient plays its part. No one ingredient is the "key ingredient". All the ingredients work together. I recommend you don't remove ingredients but please feel free to adjust quantities to suit. And add your own special ingredients. If you don't have all the ingredients now, make the best with what you've got. And then work towards finding any missing ingredients. Be the chef not a cook!

Your value is the sum of the decisions you make and the actions you take. It starts with you, but it's not all about you. Make decisions. Take action. Add value.

It's simple! *Simple as PQRST And U.*

PART 1: Clarity of Purpose (P, Q)

The purpose of this book is to provide you a simple and easy to recall recipe to improve decision-making and action taking. Why? Because your value is the sum of the decisions you make and the actions you take. With that clarity of purpose in mind, let's get started with your recipe.

Decisions are made by all people, all the time. In your organization decisions are not just made by your Board and Executive. Your Board may make "the big decisions", but the weight of those decisions does not exceed the collective weight of the decisions made by all others in your organization. To draw an analogy, in the world's oceans, the combined mass of minute plankton far exceeds the combined mass of all the big whales. And the whales are probably more dependent on plankton than the other way around!

Poor corporate culture is the consequence of poor decision-making. Or is it the other way around?

Corporate culture is difficult to define. It is "complex". And many scavenge on the carcass of corporate culture complexity – the new breed of culture vultures!

Often, corporate culture is described, rather blurrily, by "what it's like to work around here." The Board and the CEO are faced with the task of setting the culture of the organization. Easier said than done! And generally, not done well!

Let's set aside trying to define corporate culture for a minute and ask - of the many publicized failures in corporate culture, were there any that were **not** a consequence of poor decision-making?

Clearly, improving decision-making, at all levels of an organization, will reap tremendous benefits. So then, how does one improve decision-making? To find out, let's first understand what causes poor decision-making.

"There are two main causes of poor decision making: insufficient motivation and cognitive biases."

John Beshears and Francesca Gino

Poor decision-making is mainly caused by inadequate motivation and cognitive biases. It stands to reason that improving motivation and understanding cognitive biases will improve decision-making.

According to Daniel Pink, the elements of motivation are purpose, mastery, and autonomy. This Part 1 provides the ingredients for Clarity of Purpose (P, Q). The ingredients of mastery, or getting fit for purpose, are added in Part 2: Fit for Purpose (R, S, T). Part 3: And U, adds your unique ingredients and also shows how autonomy and cognitive biases contribute to the recipe.

Let's start. P is for…

P is for Purpose

> *"Purpose is the key to motivation—and motivated employees are the key to realizing your purpose. Get this symbiotic relationship right, and your organization will thrive."*
> Sally Blount and Paul Leinwand

Purpose is the reason for doing something. It's why little kids always ask "Why?". They will continue to ask "Why?" until they have an answer that comforts them. "Because I say so" does not provide comfort!

In the absence of purpose, motivation suffers. Have you ever worked on a purposeless task? How did that feel? "Motivated" would probably not be the word that springs to mind!

If an activity has no purpose, then why are you doing it? An activity without purpose is obviously and simply purposeless.

If people in your organization say "I just do what I'm told", then you have a problem with clarity of purpose.

> "The purpose of a company is to engage all its stakeholders in shared and sustained value creation. In creating such value, a company serves not only its shareholders, but all its stakeholders – employees, customers, suppliers, local communities and society at large."
>
> *Klaus Schwab*

Just like Klaus Schwab, Founder and Executive Chairman of the World Economic Forum, has eloquently described, the Boards and CEOs of many organizations invest much effort in defining the purpose of their organizations. And that is good. However, that is not where clarity of purpose stops.

Organizations are made up of teams and teams are made up of individuals. It is crucial for each team to define the team's purpose and for each person to define his or her individual purpose. The purpose of the organization, the purpose of each team and the purpose of each person are not (and need not be) the same.

> "No matter one's level, industry or career, we all need to find a personal sense of meaning in what we do."
>
> *Kristi Hedges*

So then, how do you clarify your purpose? Think you (the organization), you (the team), and you (the individual). It starts with you, but it's not all about you.

Q is for the Question

P is for Purpose and Q is for the Question. The answer to the Question clarifies your purpose.

Here's the Question:
Why do you do what you do and how will you add value to the people you serve?

That is the question!
Simple? Yes. But simple is not always easy. "Soft is Hard" says Tom Peters!

You may find the search for the answer confronting. You may find your first answer does not feel right. In fact, you may take some time and several attempts to arrive at the right answer. According to root cause analysis you may have to ask, "Why?" up to five times to get to the true answer. But when you find it you will know it's right.

Purpose Question:

Why do you do what you do and how will you add value to the people you serve?

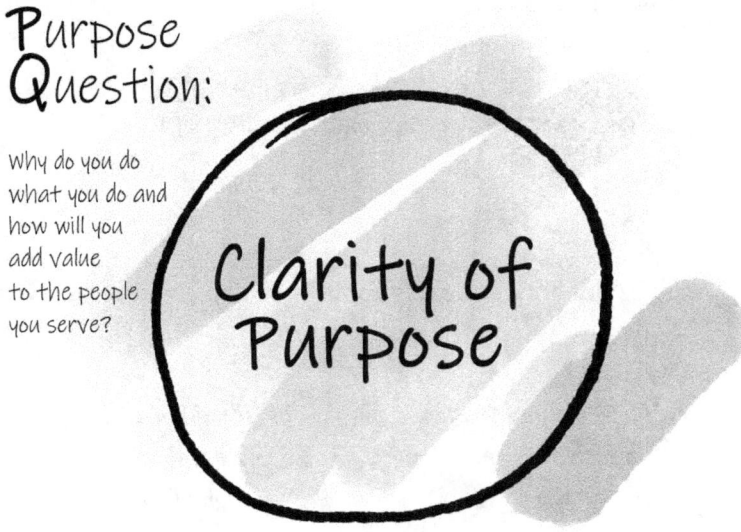

Let's look at the parts of the question.

"Why" is not how or what. This comes from Simon Sinek's Why? Why do you do what you do? It's about your motivation. Keep asking "Why?" until you find your Why.

"You" is your organization, your team (or teams), and you. Yes, you the individual. There are three perspectives of "You". Ask the question from each of the three perspectives. There's more about the three perspectives of "You" in Part 3: And U.

"And" is the essential link between what motivates you and the people you serve. Omitting "and" is simple self-indulgence!

"Value" is anything that improves the situation. People are motivated by value. To borrow a concept from my friend Todd Hutchison, think of value as a move towards gain or away from pain. Or, put another way, value is gaining a benefit or avoiding

a loss. How will you add value? If an activity does not or will not add value, then why do it at all?

> *"Strive not to be a success, but rather to be of value."*
> *Albert Einstein*

"Serve" is not about you. It's about the people you serve. Now and in the future.

> *"If I believe that as a leader, my people should be serving me, then I'm not going to be able to serve them."*
> *John C. Maxwell*

> *"Life's most persistent and urgent question is, 'What are you doing for others?'"*
> *Martin Luther King Jr.*

On the 16th of October 2019, Eliud Kipchoge made history in Vienna when he became the first human to run the standard marathon of 42.2 kilometers in under two hours, a feat once considered impossible. His time was 1hr 59min 40sec. And his fastest kilometer was the final kilometer as he picked up pace to smash through the barrier. Shortly afterwards, in the post-event interview, he said his purpose in achieving his incredible feat was motivated by his wish to serve others.

> "To inspire many people...
> to tell people no human is limited."
>
> Eliud Kipchoge

It is said there are two jobs in any company – those that serve customers and those that serve those who serve customers! From this comes the concept of the internal customer because not all jobs interact with the paying customer. Operations management theory refers to the customer as being the next person in the process. Rather, think more broadly. Think of each person you interact with as a customer. Think in all directions. Think about "the people you serve". As a simple example, think about a restaurant. Think about the role of the waiter. The waiter does not only serve the paying customer. The waiter also serves others, including the chef, who appreciates receiving feedback from the paying customer via the waiter.

Who are the people you serve? Who should you be serving? Who should you **not** be serving? Answering these questions is an important part in clarifying your purpose.

Why do you do what you do and how will you add value to the people you serve? If you're the CEO, ask the question from the perspective of your company. Find the purpose of your company. Find clarity of purpose. Also, with your executive team, clarify your executive team's purpose. And, importantly, ask the question from your perspective, as an individual, to clarify your personal purpose. Set the example and encourage everyone in your company to do the same exercise from the company's perspective, their team's perspective, and from their own perspective as an individual.

Similarly, if you're a team leader, work with your team to clarify purpose from the three perspectives.

With clarity of purpose each person sees where they fit in and how they add value. How motivating is that! Simple as!

You may not find the answer to the Question quickly or easily. Andy Kahle is a graphic artist and the illustrator of **Simple as PQRST And U**. When meeting to discuss the illustrations, I noticed Andy had a great answer to the Question on her business card. Andy said it took her some time and several attempts before she got it right. But when she got it right, she knew it was right!

"Combining skills & passion to provide unique Design, Branding & Graphics."

Andy Kahle

The answer to the question need not be long. My oldest daughter, Hannah, makes wearable silicone mermaid tails. I thought I would test her with the Question. Almost immediately she gave me one of the best answers I have heard.

> *"I make mermaid tails because I like seeing the smiles on little kids' faces."*
>
> Hannah Wells

I have often been asked what my answer to the Question is. When working with one of my clients, a medium sized civil engineering company, I made a point of getting to know each person in the business. On one occasion I asked one of the young civil engineers how he was going. He said "I'm going well! You know what, you make me feel good about doing what I do!" That comment clarified my answer to the Question.

I like it when people say, "You make me feel good about doing what I do."

Part 1 Takeaways

Why do you do what you do and how will you add value to the people you serve?

The answer to the first part of the question, "Why do you do what you do?" is driven by a move towards gain or away from pain - from your perspective. Likewise, when thinking about the value you will add to the people you serve, that value is also created by a move towards gain or away from pain from the perspective of the people you serve.

The answer to the question is about what motivates you and what motivates the people you serve. Remember, it starts with you, but it's not all about you.

Start your recipe with Clarity of Purpose. Simple as!

> *"Begin with the end in mind."*
> *Stephen R. Covey*

Next, with Clarity of Purpose, let's get Fit for Purpose.

Reader Notes:

PART 2: Fit for Purpose (R, S, T)

Having clarified purpose in Part 1, this Part 2 adds the mastery ingredients to get you in shape to fulfil your purpose. Think about what Eliud Kipchoge had to do to fulfil his purpose. Let's get Fit for Purpose.

For simplicity, the Fit for Purpose ingredients start with R, S and T. Serendipity and the versatility of the English language have allowed this to happen.

The order of the Fit for Purpose ingredients in this book have not been listed in order of importance or relevance. The order is up to you. Be guided by your Clarity of Purpose. Remember, it starts with you, but it's not all about you!

When assessing the importance of an ingredient, ask yourself, "If I had this ingredient, how would that make me feel and how would that affect me fulfilling my purpose?" And "If this ingredient was missing, how would that make me feel and how would that affect me fulfilling my purpose?"

Purpose Question:

Why do you do what you do and how will you add value to the people you serve?

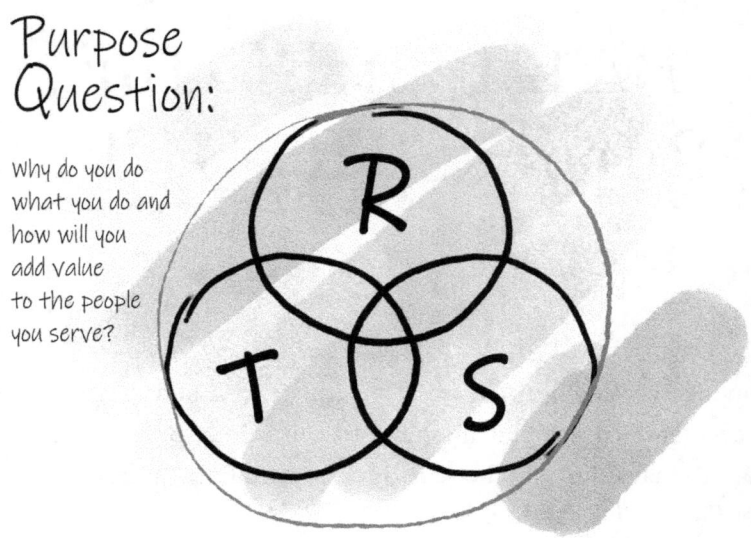

You may find you have more than enough of some ingredients but not enough of others. That gives you an opportunity to save ingredients for later or to swap and share ingredients. You may think of other ingredients you have or need. Make a mental note of those for Part 3: And U.

Let's have a look at the Fit for Purpose ingredients.

R is for...

Respect

Respect is a reciprocal relationship. Robert Cialdini identified Reciprocity as one of his six basic principles of winning friends and influencing people. People repay in kind. The Principle of Reciprocity also applies to other **Simple as PQRST And U** ingredients, such as share, support and trust. Give and you will receive. Be the first mover.

Pay respect to earn respect. It starts with you, but it's not all about you.

> *"How you treat the one reveals how you regard the many, because everyone is ultimately a one."*
> *Stephen R. Covey*

Realistic

Be a realistic optimist. Heidi Grant Halvorson, in her book *9 Things Successful People do Differently*, found that people who believed they would succeed in a task and believed it would be difficult, were more likely to succeed in that task than those who believed they would succeed and believed it would be easy. It's not Easy as. It's Simple as!

Resources

Resources include physical things such as a decent computer screen at your workstation, or an oven if you're a chef, or iron ore if you're a miner. Resources also include financial resources to buy the things you need to fulfil your purpose.

I prefer not to categorise people as resources. People are not like a body of iron ore! In this recipe, all the ingredients combine to getting the right people for your purpose.

Resources are finite. You will probably not have all the resources you would ideally like to fulfil your purpose. Be clear on what resources you have and what you need (as opposed to want). Rank your resources in order of importance. What is essential? What could you do without? What do you need that you don't have? What do you have that you don't need? Swap surplus resources for the resources you need. Be guided by your Clarity of Purpose.

Reward

What do you get in return for providing value to the people you serve? Reward comes in many forms. And each person will have their preference of how they would like to be rewarded. Often simple recognition is a great motivator. Money may not be the ultimate motivator but if you do not get paid at the end of the month for your efforts you will probably not feel motivated! What is certain is that the absence of reward is de-motivating.

> *"Recognition is a fundamental human need. At the most basic level, it makes us feel valued, which is what inspires us to stay all bright-eyed and bushy-tailed at work."*
> Vartika Kashyap

Reward is necessary for sustainability. You will not survive for long without reward. If you are providing value, you deserve your reward! Do not be embarrassed about receiving your reward. And reward is necessary for you to continue to provide value to the people you serve.

Are you receiving appropriate reward for providing value to the people you serve? Are you providing enough value for the reward you receive? It starts with you, but it's not all about you.

> *"Value is not determined by those who set the price. Value is determined by those who choose to pay it."*
> Simon Sinek

Risk

The risk reward relationship says that zero risk equates to zero reward. Simple as!

Take the risk of trusting those you lead. You will be rewarded.

Concerningly, the Australian Institute of Company Directors found that 71 percent of its members describe their Boards as "Risk averse".

> *"True strategy is about placing bets and making hard choices. The objective of strategy is not to minimise risk but to increase the chance of success."*
>
> Roger Martin

Get **Simple as PQRST And U** right and you will be equipped to handle risk and receive the reward for doing so.

Resilience

Steven Bradbury is famous for becoming Australia's first Winter Olympics Gold Medalist. *Last Man Standing* is his story. It is a story of overcoming adversity over many years. It is a story of resilience. Without resilience Steven would not have won Olympic gold at his fourth Olympics.

I have heard Steven tell his story a couple of times and would gladly hear it again. One of the things he does is to allow his gold medal to be passed around the audience. The medal is a lot heavier than you would expect! I also noticed what is engraved on the back of the medal.

After the first time I heard Steven present his story I bought a copy of his book and, along with many others, lined up to have the book autographed. For each person Steven took the trouble to write a personalized message. When my turn came, he asked me what message I would like him to write. I asked him to write what is engraved on the back of his gold medal. Without a word but with a knowing smile he wrote: "Light the Fire Within". Resilience is keeping the fire burning within. Simple as!

Renewal

Are you keeping yourself in shape to achieve your purpose? Are you taking time to exercise well, eat well and sleep well? Are you keeping a healthy mind, body, and soul? Are you keeping your relationships healthy?

Keep yourself in shape to achieve your purpose. The same applies to your teams, and your business.

> *"The self-renewal process must include balanced renewal in all four dimensions of our nature: the physical, the spiritual, the mental, and the social/emotional."*
>
> Stephen R. Covey

Role

Serial Entrepreneur Alan Nelson found himself struggling with how he could add most value to his portfolio of businesses. He looked to his mentor for advice.

"You enjoy your football, don't you?" said Alan's mentor. "Err, yes" said Alan, wondering how that was relevant.

"Picture a football field. Picture the players on the field, each in their positions. Picture the captain of the team. Picture the coach of the team. Picture the fans. Picture the Manager. Picture the support staff. Picture the owner of the team," said Alan's mentor. "Each person has an important role to play in the team." "Now think about you and your businesses. Are you a player, the captain, the coach, the manager, one of the support staff, one of the fans, or are you the owner?". Alan realized that he had been on the metaphorical playing field when his role was that of the owner of his businesses.

Be clear on your role and where you add most value. And if you lead a team, it is your responsibility to assist your team to find roles where each person can be their best.

Relationships

To borrow another concept, from my friend Todd Hutchison, people do business with people they know, like and trust. Building relationships is a great way to build business! More broadly, building relationships is a great way to achieve your purpose.

Ask yourself, "Which relationships are most important in achieving your purpose?" Clearly, nurturing your relationships with those who are near and dear to you is important in achieving your purpose. But what about those relationships that are less dear to you? What about relationships with people or organizations you may not particularly like? Take your industry's regulators as an example. And what about relationships with people or organizations who do not like you? Remember, value is added by making a move towards gain or away from pain. So, improving a relationship from bad to satisfactory can be significant in achieving your purpose. In fact, it may be more significant than moving a relationship from good to great!

Responsibility

Who is responsible for each of the ingredients of your recipe? Who is best positioned to find and add the ingredients? If you're thinking, "I am!", you're right! It starts with you, but it's not all about you.

Do you take responsibility? Or do you avoid responsibility? Remember it starts with you, but it's not all about you. Yes, taking responsibility comes with risk. But with risk, comes reward. Be responsible. Take responsibility. You will be rewarded!

Reflect

> *"It is by three methods we may learn wisdom: First, by reflection, which is noblest; second, by imitation, which is easiest; and third by experience, which is the bitterest."*
>
> *Confucius*

Gain wisdom through noble reflection! What did you do well? What would you do differently next time? Learn from the past. Learn what to do. And what not to do!

> "Life is both beautiful and messy and this is your learning opportunity and your path."
>
> Lisa McCarthy FAIM

> "Life can only be understood backwards; but it must be lived forwards."
>
> Søren Kierkegaard

Review

Review is not rear view. Review is not about looking backwards. Review is taking a fresh view. Review is looking into the future. It's about making sure the ingredients of your recipe are fresh.

While writing **Simple as PQRST And U**, I made a point of applying **Simple as PQRST And U** along the way. When thinking about Review, I changed Q, the Question, from "Why do you do what you do and how **do** you add value to the people you serve?" to "Why do you do what you do and how **will** you add value to the people you serve?". That decision to change Q, the Question, from a past and current perspective to a future perspective followed my attending a presentation by Gihan Perera, author of Disruption by Design.

> "...map the future customer's journey, because you can then identify how to serve future customers and their needs."
>
> Gihan Perera

Gihan Perara, tells a story about Albert Einstein. When Einstein was asked why he set the same exam question to his students year after year, he replied:

> *"The question is the same, but the answer is different."*
> *Albert Einstein*

Why do you do what you do and how will you add value to the people you serve? The question is the same, but the answer will change. Your role may change. Your company's owners may change. Your customer's needs may change. Your situation may change.

> *"The only thing that is constant is change."*
> *Heraclitus*

Change has been around for a while, as Heraclitus pointed out centuries ago; but the rate of change has increased. And continues to increase.

> *"... it is not the most intellectual of the species that survives; it is not the strongest that survives; but the species that survives is the one that is able best to adapt and adjust to the changing environment in which it finds itself."*
> *Leon C. Megginson (Not Charles Darwin!)*

Review your purpose regularly because things change and can change quickly. Be 'change able'

Soon after the outbreak of the COVID-19 pandemic, the shelves were cleared of hand sanitizer. 'Change able' boutique gin distillers responded to the situation and started to produce boutique hand sanitizer. On 1 April 2020, that was the reality. On 1 April 2019, the idea would have been dismissed as an April Fool prank!

S is for...

Situation

Do you have the appropriate level of information to understand the situation adequately? When making decisions, beware of analysis paralysis at one extreme and impulse at the opposite extreme. Are you more inclined towards analysis paralysis or are you an impulsive decision-maker? How about others in your team? How do they see you?

It is important to appreciate the difference between data and information. Information is the result from processing, structuring, organising and presenting data in a useful way. There is no shortage of data. The increasing volume of data is causing data blindness. People can't see the information wood for the data trees! Relevant, reliable, and accurate information is what you need to understand a situation.

Don't wait for perfect information. Sometimes perfect information may arrive too late. Don't allow perfection to get in the way of greatness.

Sometimes problems are difficult or even impossible to define. These are known as wicked problems. In these circumstances it is particularly important to get a clear understanding of the situation. With others, find a shared understanding of the situation. And then try different things. Even if just one at a time. That way you can see if what you're trying improves the situation.

> *"Earn the right to be heard by listening to others. Seek to understand a situation before making judgments about it."*
>
> John C. Maxwell

Are you seeing the situation the way it is or is it being clouded by your opinion and beliefs? If you want to understand reality, distinguish between what is an opinion or a belief and what is fact.

> *"Being always in favor of or always against a particular idea makes you blind to information that doesn't fit your perspective. This is usually a bad approach if you would like to understand reality."*
>
> Hans Rosling

Sometimes actions to improve the situation in one area have adverse impacts in another area. The COVID-19 Pandemic created what Australian Prime Minister, Scott Morrison, called a dual crisis. A simultaneous health crisis and economic crisis. Taking measures to address the health crisis would have adverse implications for the economy. A classic situation of being on the horns of a dilemma. By avoiding either one of the horns the Prime Minister would be impaled by the other horn.

> *"A decision without the pressure of consequence is hardly a decision at all."*
>
> Eric Langmuir

Space

Find your decision space. It's a place where you have clarity of mind to make decisions. It's more about a clear state of mind, than a physical place. You may find it while doing your exercise routine or some other activity that allows your mind to relax. Get to know when you're in your decision space. And, equally importantly, get to know when you are not.

Find a way of recalling that clarity of thought found in your decision space. I often use voice memos on my phone to record an idea if I don't have a pen at hand or I'm not at my computer. Many of those voice memos have found a place in ***Simple as PQRST And U***.

Skills

Do you like doing something because you are good at it, or are you good at it because you like doing it? That's probably a chicken and egg question. However, having the right skills certainly makes things easier and more enjoyable. The great thing about skills is that you can acquire new ones and develop existing ones. And if the going gets tough, you can improve your skills.

> *"Smooth seas do not make skillful sailors."*
> African proverb

Share

Share your purpose with others. If you have nailed your purpose, your Clarity of Purpose will energise others to assist you in fulfilling your purpose. The Principle of Reciprocity applies again.

While writing this book I shared my purpose and received encouragement and ideas in return. Frequently, I shared my thoughts with Greg Bridge, one of my regular golf partners. Greg had just published his first book, *Yes*. I knew that before we teed up Greg was going to ask me how I was progressing with ***Simple as PQRST And U***. He had made it his purpose to make sure I kept writing and to get ***Simple as PQRST And U*** published.

So, share your purpose. Share the purpose of your team. Share the purpose of your business. If you share your purpose with others, they will help you get there. Think about advertising your business as sharing your purpose.

> "Doing business without advertising is like winking at a girl in the dark. You know what you're doing but nobody else does!"
>
> — Steuart Henderson Britt

You may find you have more than enough of some ingredients but not enough of other ingredients. Share with others. And they will share with you. Sharing is what makes us human.

> "We are human because our ancestors learned to share their food and their skills in an honored network of obligation."
>
> — Richard Leakey

Support

To support is motivating. To have supporters is motivating. Reciprocity applies again!

Be a mentor (provide support). Have a mentor (seek support). It's a mutually beneficial relationship.

Seek support. Do not be too modest to seek support. When asked, people are usually willing and pleased to help. It's in our nature. Ask and you shall receive.

> "Seek and you shall find."
>
> — The Bible, Matthew 7:7-8

Provide support. Be there when needed. You will be rewarded.

> *"If we fail to look after others when they need help, who will look after us?"*
>
> Buddha

In post-match interviews, how often have you heard the competitors thanking their supporters? "We couldn't have done it without you" they say. To have supporters is motivating. And if you support a team that does well, how good does that make you feel? To support is motivating.

Strategy

Purpose and strategy are, or should be, closely aligned. In a business context, strategy is about finding ways to create value for the people you serve in a way that is sustainable to your business. If you're not doing that, you're not doing strategy.

> *"The role of the CEO is first and foremost to validate the link between a company's strategy and its purpose."*
>
> Jean-Dominique Senard

Because things change, doing more of the same is not strategy. Business as usual is the enemy of strategy. Step away from business as usual when preparing your strategy.

Because resources are finite, you can't do everything. Strategy requires decisions about what to do and what not to do.

Scenarios

Picturing scenarios, including unlikely ones, equips you with the benefit of hindsight in the event they materialize. Call it foresight if you wish! If you have developed various scenarios you will be alert to the early signals that a scenario is developing and you can make the appropriate decisions, simply because you've been there before.

> *"The best leaders use the benefit of foresight to make better decisions – and faster – even in an uncertain, ever-changing world."*
>
> Gihan Perera

Standards

Some years back, when working for a company providing serviced workforce accommodation, I was showing a prospective customer around our accommodation village at Karratha, Western Australia. Our Village Manager, Bradley, was leading the way as we walked through the village, which was looking neat and tidy as usual. As we were nearing the end of the walk-around, Bradley spotted a cigarette butt in one of the garden beds next to the foot path and he picked it up. That cigarette butt would not have been noticed by the prospective customer. But she noticed that Bradley noticed. Bradley set the standard by not walking past. And we were awarded a significant accommodation contract.

The standard you walk past is the standard you set. Actions speak louder than words.

Safety

This is not just about hard hats and high viz vests. It's about feeling safe to say what needs to be said. And, if you're a leader, your role is to create a safe space for people to say what needs to be said.

> *"Be a brave and courageous thinker. Speak the truth to power. Be the voice of dissent. Dissent is not disloyalty."*
> Mario D'Orazio

Systems

Set up systems, processes, and procedures for repetitive, routine activities to free up time for creativity and making big decisions. Review your systems, processes, and procedures to check alignment with your purpose. Do they and will they add value to the people you serve? If not, get rid of them or change them. Keep it simple. Simple as!

Start

Congratulations on reaching this point! You clearly decided to read **Simple as PQRST And U**. Importantly, you also started. And that was when your chances of finishing the book increased dramatically!

Simple as PQRST And U is about improving your value by making decisions and taking action. Remember a bias for action?

> "Act or be acted upon."
> Stephen R. Covey

Procrastination is a symptom of lack of Clarity of Purpose or not being Fit for Purpose or both. Recall Steven Covey's, "Begin with the end in mind?" Start by clarifying your purpose. If you don't start, you are guaranteed not to finish.

You may feel your Clarity of Purpose is not perfectly clear. Remember, it's not necessarily easy.

Don't delay the start. You can always change direction once you've started. Review allows you to revisit your purpose and to tweak it.

Do not allow fear of failure to prevent you from starting. You may not yet be fully Fit for Purpose, but you won't get fit while lying on the couch!

Don't wait for perfection. Don't allow perfection to get in the way. My friend and golfing buddy, Greg Bridge, gave me a tip while writing **Simple as PQRST And U**: "Don't wait for perfection before publishing your book."

Don't allow doubt to spoil your recipe!

> *"Doubts are a nasty beast; inside your brain they like to feast."*
>
> Anon

Jim Collins talks about the flywheel effect. It takes effort to get the flywheel started but once it gets going, the momentum builds, people feel the momentum, and will line up with enthusiasm.

One of the reasons we avoid starting something new is that there is almost always a dip in performance after starting something new. It is best illustrated by the Sigmoid curve, also known as the S-curve. Performance dips initially after the start, before it picks up again. The trick is to minimise the extent and duration of the dip. Then ride the wave of increasing performance.

Inevitably, because things change, the performance wave will lose momentum. Before it does, start again and catch the next wave. And so on. **Simple as PQRST And U** will help you to work out when to make your move.

If you want to have the time to do what you want to do, first start with doing what you need to do.
How about starting with **Simple as PQRST And U?**

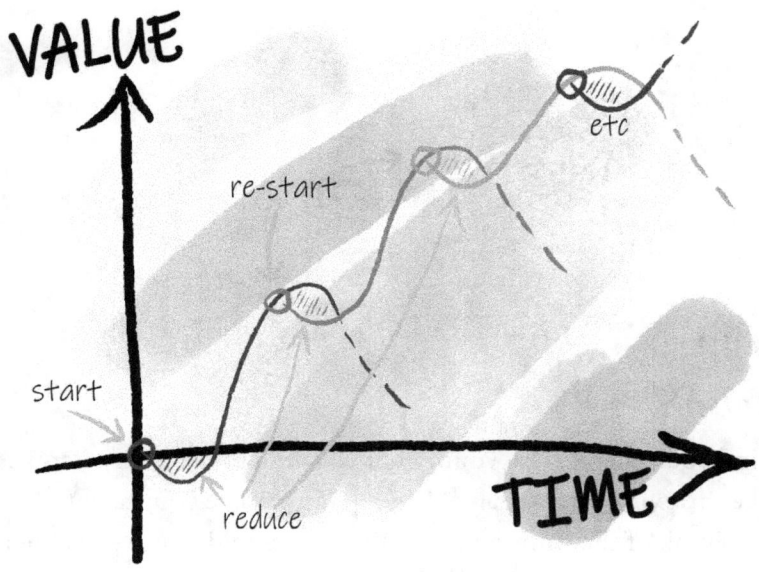

T is for...

Talent

Find your talents. Use your talents. Failing to use your talents is like throwing away a valuable gift. Don't waste your talents.

Think of the things where others have said you are talented. Particularly, if said by different people in different circumstances.

What talents, skills, knowledge, and experience do you have that others don't know about? Find an opportunity to demonstrate them. Don't hide them. Don't assume others know.

> "Surprisingly often, people mistakenly assume that others recognize and appreciate their experience."
> Robert Cialdini

Training

Athletes do not get fit without training and practice. In the same way, it is necessary to train to get Fit for Purpose. The fitter you get the better you will perform. Your motivation will improve and that will increase your performance, which will motivate you further. And so on. Simple as!

> *"The more I practice the luckier I get."*
> Gary Player

Practice *Simple as PQRST And U*.

Tools and techniques

Do you have the right tools for your trade? And do you know how to use them?

For example, a physiotherapist needs a physio bench. And needs to know how to use it!

Imagine, you're on holiday with the family at the coast and you've decided to take a day trip in your new 4x4 to explore a river mouth some 10 kilometers along a remote beach. You have loaded up the vehicle with kayaks, fishing gear, picnic basket, drinks, sunscreen, and the whole family.

Halfway to the destination you hit a patch of soft sand and your vehicle gets stuck up to the axle. And the tide is coming in!

Just when you had thought your new 4x4 would be lost to King Neptune, another 4x4 appeared with an experienced driver equipped with traction mats (the right tools). He deflated the tyres (the right technique), positioned the traction mats under the wheels, and you were going again.

Having the right tools and techniques for the purpose may not necessarily be motivating but not having them when you need them, is certainly demotivating.

The Australian Institute of Management WA regularly holds the Inspirational Leaders Series. I am a regular attendee and have learnt from the speakers and fellow attendees at these events. The breakfasts are great too!

At one of the events, while enjoying breakfast ahead of the presentation, I was chatting with Alan Fairhead, one of the regular attendees at the Leadership Series. At the time, I was halfway through writing *Simple as PQRST And U* and we were talking about the book. I had briefly run through the concept and thought I would explain the application of Techniques by analogy to the juicy cooked cherry tomatoes on my breakfast plate. These cherry tomatoes were delicious. However, they were as slippery as greased marbles and difficult to hold on a fork. They also ejected tomato juice when pierced with a fork! I explained to Alan that I needed to refine my cherry tomato technique to avoid spending breakfast steering the tomatoes around my plate or squirting myself, or worse, squirting someone else in the eye with tomato juice! Alan's response was perfect. "You don't have to use a fork. How about using a spoon?"

Simple as PQRST And U is a decision-making tool. Take it with you wherever you go. And practice using the tool to improve your technique. You will be amazed how lucky you get!

Technology

Technology is also a tool. In choosing the appropriate technology, always keep your purpose in mind. Ask "How will this technology add value?" Constantly think of how technology can add value to the people you serve.

> *"Data is the new natural resource, so you need to think, 'now that I've aggregated that, how do I get something useful out of it?'"*
>
> Doug Robinson

Natalie Nguyen is the CEO of Hyper Anna, which Natalie describes as being an entirely artificial intelligence data scientist clone of herself. Natalie uses Hyper Anna to handle repetitive data analysis so she can focus on higher thinking. Natalie sees artificial intelligence creating an exciting future workplace where we can spend more time using our business acumen and moral compass to make better decisions.

> *"It is just another tool. A very powerful tool, but still a tool. You need people to make decisions."*
>
> Natalie Nguyen

IBM is a world leader in artificial intelligence technology. Interestingly and importantly, IBM has Clarity of Purpose. Purpose is not diluted by artificial intelligence technology.

> "Problems inspire us to push the world forward. IBM is changing the way the world works by applying smart technologies at scale, with purpose and expertise. Smart loves problems. Let's put smart to work. ®"
>
> IBM

Trust

Trust is coupled with respect. Pay respect to others and earn trust in return. The Principle of Reciprocity again! Trust others and they will trust you. It starts with you, but it's not all about you.

Having clarified purpose and gotten Fit for Purpose, trust yourself and your team to perform. Because perform you will. Perhaps not perfectly, but definitely better than before. And that will be motivating, which will make you and your team perform even better! Simple as!

Tasks

Are you clear on what you must do and when? Do you have a list of tasks to do today? And a list of what you need to achieve in the next 30 days? Write down what you need to do. Your to do list. It can be in your good old paper notebook or on an electronic device. The act of writing is a commitment to yourself, which increases the chance of it happening. Also, sharing your targets with others increases your motivation to get things done.

Making progress on meaningful work is one of our strongest motivators. So, as you complete each task, even if you have not done all you set out to do, tick off your completed tasks. That will give you a sense of accomplishment. And then carry over incomplete tasks to your to do list for tomorrow.

Daniel Pink suggests a technique he attributes to Warren Buffet. Write down the 25 most important things you need to do to achieve your purpose. Then, identify the five most important of those 25 things. Set aside the other 20 and focus on doing the top five. Only look at the other 20 when you've completed all the top five.

One of my favorite tools for prioritizing tasks is the urgent/important matrix. Put each of your tasks into one of the matrix quadrants. Start with those in the Priority Zone quadrant. These are your highest priority. Next, be selective on the tasks in the Selective Zone and do those. Delegate these tasks if you can. Don't get bogged down on tasks in the Selective Zone. Afterall, they are not of high importance. Then, with the burden of urgency lifted, you can focus on the more important tasks in the Quality Zone. If you follow this approach consistently you will find you are spending less time putting out fires in the urgent zones and more time making good decisions and taking action in the Quality Zone. And you will have time for some self-indulgence in the Optional Zone.

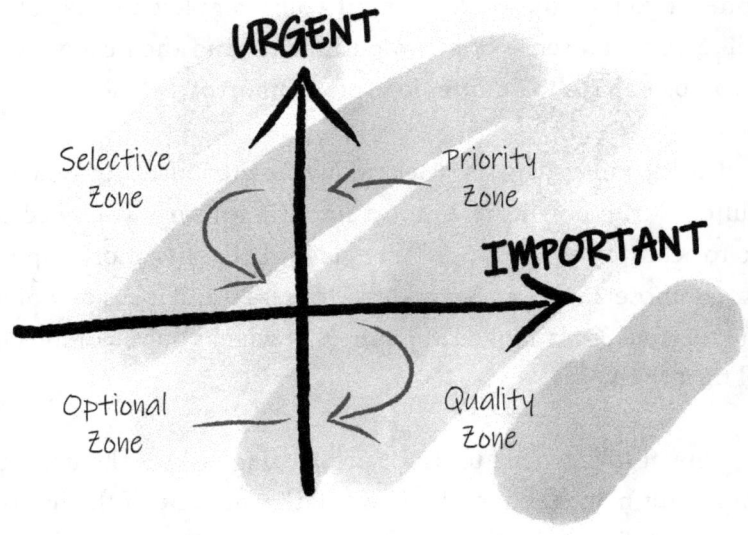

Your value is the sum of the decisions you make **and** the actions you take. The emphasis on **and** is deliberate. Make decisions **and** take action.

Team

Great teams do great things. Being part of a successful team is a tremendous motivator. A successful team is one where the team produces more than the sum of the individual contributions.

"...a team like this - we come from different backgrounds, different races - came together with one goal. I really hope we have done that

for South Africa, to show that we can pull together if we want to achieve something."

Siya Kolisi

"The whole is greater than the sum of its parts."

Aristotle

Diversity of skills, styles and thoughts are the special ingredients that help a team to produce more than the sum of the individual contributions.

Equity and inclusion plans are often dressed up as diversity. Equity and inclusion are about respect and fairness and the benefit is not limiting your talent pool. The reality is that equity and inclusion do not assure an effectively diverse team.

If you choose team members who see things in a way similar to you, your team is likely to see the same things and not see the same things. It's what you do not see as a team that is likely to be your pitfall or an opportunity missed.

There are easily accessible tools available to assess how balanced your team is and how each person can contribute most effectively to your team. One of the most useful is Belbin® Team Roles, which identifies nine team roles from the work of Dr Meredith Belbin and his team.

> "A team is not a bunch of people with job titles, but a congregation of individuals, each of whom has a role which is understood by other members."
>
> Belbin®

Think

Nobel Prize Winner, Daniel Kahneman talks about thinking fast and thinking slow.

Thinking fast is what an impala applies when it glimpses the twitch of a lion's ear in the grass. Or when a cricketer decides to play or duck a 100 miles per hour bouncer. Thinking fast draws on instinct. The effectiveness of the fast thinking response is improved by picturing scenarios and proper training. That's why good cricketers practice before facing fast bowling.

Thinking slow is more deliberate and reasoned. It's when you have time to gather your thoughts.

The best decisions are made when the appropriate thinking mode is applied to the situation.

Think forwards (Review) but learn from the past (Reflect). Don't bury spontaneous thought. Use it as a catalyst. Give crazy ideas time to germinate. They may grow into great things.

Think big early. It is easy to trim later if necessary. My youngest daughter, Nicola loves performing on stage. When she was 12, we went to a performance at her prospective high school's theater. "Dad, she said. "This stage is too small for me. I was born to be on the big stage!". Thinking big early! And now

I'm the Convenor of the school's new theatre building committee!

Edward de Bono's Six Thinking Hats is a technique that can be applied to look at things from different perspectives. In a similar way, three different hats should be worn when applying **Simple as PQRST And U**. The hat of you, the individual. The hat of you, the team. The hat of you, the business. Each hat provides a different perspective.

No matter how much we flatter ourselves, the reality is that our thinking as individuals has limitations. Individually, as much as we may try, we can't see all perspectives perfectly. Fortunately, if we harness the thoughts of people who think differently and therefor see things differently, the picture becomes clearer. That's diversity of thought. That's what adds value.

Timing

Some decisions need to be made quickly. Like the impala or the cricketer. For others we may have the benefit of time to arrive at a decision. The key is to make the right decision at the right time. That's timing.

> *"I used to believe that timing was everything. Now I believe that everything is timing."*
>
> *Daniel Pink*

Thanks

Be grateful for what you have. Give thanks.
And thank those around you. It makes them feel appreciated. And that is motivating for them. And for you too.

While working at a local restaurant, my daughter Hannah, noticed a policeman on night shift had ordered a takeaway burger. She prepared the burger and placed it in the takeaway box. Then she wrote a message on the box, "Thank you for your service." Later that evening the policeman posted on the restaurant's Facebook page: "Thanks for an amazing burger – it tasted fantastic. And for the really nice message. It really made my night".

Thank you for reading *Simple as PQRST And U*.

Part 2 Takeaways

Serendipity, combined with the versatility of the English language, have allowed the Fit for Purpose ingredients to conveniently start with R or S or T. The order of these ingredients is not relevant. Some of the ingredients can be grouped if you like. Such as, for example, Respect and Trust. And Talent, Skills and Training. And Resources, Tools and Technology. However, all the ingredients are linked. 'And' is the link that binds the ingredients. And if you don't have all the ingredients, make the best with what you've got in the meantime. This is your recipe. Be the chef, not the cook!

Next, we show how the ingredients combine and where you fit in!

Reader Notes:

PART 3: And U

Part 1 starts with the ingredients to find Clarity of Purpose (P, Q). Part 2 adds the ingredients to get Fit for Purpose (R, S, T). This Part 3 adds your unique ingredients, shows how the ingredients combine, explains the importance of U (the organization), U (the team) and U (the individual), and reinforces that it starts with you, but it's not all about you.

Purpose Question:

Why do you do what you do and how will you add value to the people you serve?

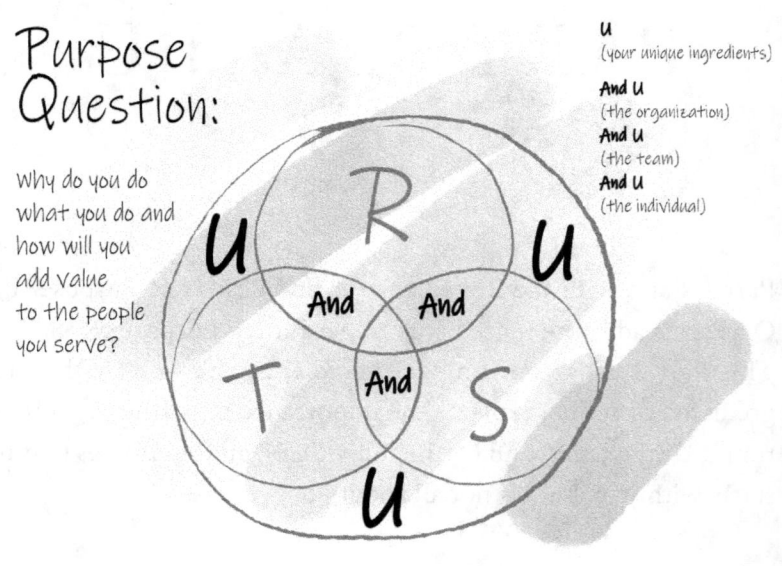

U
(your unique ingredients)

And U
(the organization)
And U
(the team)
And U
(the individual)

The Power of And

*Why do you do what you do **and** how will you add value to the people you serve?* That is the question! The answer is your purpose.

The emphasis on '**and**' is deliberate. It's not 'or'. The first part of the question is about your motivation, the second part is about what motivates the people you serve.

Peter Drucker is well known for what became known as Management by Objectives, often abbreviated to MBO. Three letter acronyms are annoying. Darn TLAs!

Originally, Drucker's concept was Management by Objectives **and** Self-control. Somewhere along the line "and Self-control" went missing. And MBO fell out of favour. Don't lose the power of And!

Each of the ingredients of ***Simple as PQRST And U*** contribute to the recipe. And binds the ingredients together. It's And, not Or.

And what about you? This is where you can add your own unique ingredients to the recipe. Customize the recipe. It's your recipe. Be the chef, not the cook!

What are your unique ingredients that will contribute towards fulfilling your purpose? Write them down and add them to your recipe.

Treble U

Purpose, mastery and autonomy are the key elements of motivation. We clarified purpose in Part 1: Clarity of Purpose (P, Q). We added the ingredients of mastery in Part 2: Fit for Purpose (R, S, T). Now let's find out what autonomy adds to the recipe.

Autonomy stems from two Greek words; autos, meaning self, and nomos, meaning law. Autonomy is the right to rule or control oneself. It applies to an individual, team, organization or any group that has a need to be autonomous. Hence, Peter Drucker's Management by Objectives **and** Self-control!

Having clarity of organization purpose is important, but not sufficient. Not enough attention is given to allowing teams and individuals to clarify purpose. We all need to know where we fit in and how we add value. That need applies to us as individuals, to our teams and to our organizations. Recall Kristi Hedges' words.

> *"No matter one's level, industry or career, we all need to find a personal sense of meaning in what we do."*
>
> *Kristi Hedges*

The purpose of the organization, the purpose of each team, and the purpose of each individual should not, and need not, be the same. A 'one size fits all' organization purpose should not be imposed on teams and individuals.

If each team and each individual is not allowed to clarify purpose, then each team and each individual is denied autonomy. Wars have been caused in the quest for autonomy!

Each team and each individual must be granted autonomy to clarify purpose and develop mastery. Get that right and you have motivated teams and people. If not, you have the ingredients for an internal war! And if you have the ingredients for an internal war, you will inevitably have, to use corporate speak, a failure in corporate culture.

Treble U is about applying **Simple as PQRST And U** to U the organization, U the team, and U the individual. U and U and U.

It starts with U

So, who grants autonomy? Do you grant autonomy to the people you lead? Fear and ego get in the way.

> *"The new smart will be about trying to overcome the two big inhibitors of critical thinking and team collaboration: our ego and our fears. Doing so will make it easier to perceive reality as it is, rather than as we wish it to be."*
>
> *Ed Hess*

> *Our reflex to protect our egos never leaves us, but as we ask ourselves different questions, we can discover—and follow—a development path that enriches us as human beings and ultimately benefits our teams, organizations, and even the world."*
>
> *Jennifer Garvey Berger and Zafer Gedeon Achi*

Like trust and respect, autonomy must first be granted. Don't wait for autonomy to be earned. It starts with you. Most people get the importance of autonomy when thinking about what motivates them but are reluctant to grant autonomy. It starts with you, but it's not all about you!

The advent of artificial intelligence has not reduced the need to grant autonomy. On the contrary.

> *"In a world where artificial intelligence supports all manner of day-to-day management decisions, the need to "let go" will be more significant and the discomfort for senior leaders higher."*
> Martin Dewhurst and Paul Willmott

> *"As AI grows in power, the likelihood of sinking under the weight of even quite valuable insights grows as well. The solution would be to democratize information by encouraging business units and functions to make more and better decisions themselves."*
> McKinsey Classics / January 2020

So, whose responsibility is it to provide Clarity of Purpose and get Fit for Purpose? It starts with you. Treble U.

The evening before the 1992 Barcelona Olympic final of the rowing coxed pair, Team GB's sports psychologist, Brian Miller, spoke with the two rowers, brothers Jonny and Greg Searle and cox Garry Herbert. Brian Miller recounted the words Sergey Bubka's coach said to Bubka just before Bubka's third and final attempt to clear 5.90 metres in the pole vault final at the Seoul Olympics in 1988. Success meant Olympic gold for Bubka. Failure meant 4th place and no medal. Bubka won gold. And Team GB too.

> *"If not now, when? If not you, who?"*
>
> *Brian Miller*

My housemaster at high school, Allen Duff, was a great teacher and mentor. He was also the master of mixed metaphors. One of his classics has stuck with me ever since:

> *"The ball is in your court. Just keep it off the wickets!"*
>
> *Allen Duff*

It's not all about U

It's not all about you. It's about the people you serve and how you will add value to them. And appreciating you can't do it alone. It's about interdependence.

Our need for autonomy is driven by our desire to be independent. Granting autonomy is a step towards interdependence.

> *"Dependent people need others to get what they want. Independent people can get what they want through their own effort. Interdependent people combine their own efforts with the efforts of others to achieve great success."*
> *Stephen R. Covey*

Stephen Covey's wise words apply to teams and businesses too. Apply Treble U to his words by simply replacing 'people' with 'teams' and then with 'businesses'.

Empathy has become part of corporate speak. Simply put, it is the ability to see things through another person's eyes.

Dr Tasha Eurich has found that people who know how others see them are more skilled at taking others' perspectives. Therefore, clearly, the ability to see things from another person's perspective is essential in working out how you will add value to the people you serve.

Self-awareness is a prerequisite to becoming skilled at seeing things from the perspective of the people you serve. Seeing yourself as who you are is the first part of self-awareness. It starts with you. Seeing how others see you is the important other part. It's not all about you. Simple? Yes. But, clearly, not easy for most of us, as Dr Tasha Eurich has found.

> *"We've found that even though most people believe they are self-aware, self-awareness is a truly rare quality: We estimate that only 10%–15% of the people we studied actually fit the criteria."*

> *"...leaders must actively work on both seeing themselves clearly and getting feedback to understand how others see them."*
>
> Dr Tasha Eurich

Your personal brand is what people say about you when you're not in the room. The same applies to your team brand and your business brand. Do you know what people say about you, your team, and your business when you're not in the room? How do you know?

There is nothing new about the benefits of self-awareness and understanding others. As Sun Wu observed centuries ago, in *The Art of War*, it's a matter of survival.

> *"If you know yourself and you also know others, you will not be endangered in a hundred battles."*
>
> Sun Wu

Think about U, the individual. If you're the CEO of your organization, it's not all about you. Encourage all people in your organization to apply **Simple as PQRST And U** at all three levels of U. And listen, as opposed to hear, to what they say. Don't allow your ego to get in the way.

If you're a team leader, it's not all about you. Encourage all people in your team to apply **Simple as PQRST And U** at all three levels of U. And listen, (as opposed to hear), to what they say. Don't allow your ego to get in the way.

The same applies to you as a team member.

> *"Listening isn't just hearing; it requires the willingness to entertain other viewpoints—especially opposing ones."*
>
> Ram Charan

Think about U, your team. It's not all about your team. It's about how your team will add value to the people your team serves.

Think about U, your business. It's not all about your business. It's about how your business will add value to the people your business serves.

Is your website all about you, or is it about what's important to the people you serve? So, your website boasts you have 10,000 employees in 50 countries. Interesting. How will that add value to the people you serve?

If you think you're a decision-maker you're correct. But you're not alone. All people make decisions. All the time. It's not all about you. Recall the plural "your" and "you"? Your value is the sum of the decisions you make and the actions you take. Quite simply, improving decision making and action taking, by all people in your teams and your business, will add value.

Simple as PQRST And U.

Blind U

You may recall that inadequate motivation and cognitive biases are the two main contributors to poor decision-making. Up to this part of the recipe we have focused on the ingredients to improve motivation. Now it's time to have a look at the mystery ingredient we all have. Cognitive biases.

The tricky thing with cognitive biases is that although you may sense they are there, they are difficult for you to see because they hide in your blind spot. They can spoil your recipe.

> *"We can be blind to the obvious, and we are also blind to our blindness."*
>
> *Daniel Kahneman*

Cognitive biases sprout from heuristics. For a degustation on heuristics and cognitive biases I can recommend Nobel Prize Winner Daniel Kahneman's book *Thinking, Fast and Slow*. This chapter of **Simple as PQRST And U** offers the equivalent of a healthy takeaway.

Heuristics are deeply ingrained mental shortcuts we use to navigate our way through the continuous waves of data we receive through our senses. They are a mechanism developed through evolution and our experiences to help us filter what we need from data bombardment. Think about one of our ancient ancestors sensing the presence of a sabre toothed tiger just in time. Compared to the one who did not! Heuristics are a survival mechanism.

Clearly, heuristics are helpful. But, as Daniel Pink says, everything is timing. At times, our heuristics filter information we do need. We do not see what we can't see. Daniel Kahneman talks about What You See Is All There Is. We base our decisions on what we can see, and this leads to cognitive biases. Each of us develop cognitive biases. And, because we are unique, we each develop a unique set of cognitive biases.

Think about *Thinking, Fast and Slow*. In the thinking fast mode, our heuristics are most active. Like a fine-grained sieve, our heuristics sieve out some of the healthy bits. In the thinking slow mode, we have time to select a coarser sieve that sieves the sticks and stones from the mix but allows through all the healthy bits. And that makes for a healthy recipe.

The first line of defense against cognitive biases is being aware they exist. Be aware you have blind spots. It starts with you. Clearly, you can't see your own blind spots. But others can. The best defense against cognitive biases is heeding feedback from others. It's not all about you.

> "Face the facts of being what you are, for that is what changes what you are."
>
> Søren Kierkegaard

There are many cognitive biases that affect our decision making. John Beshears and Francesca Gino, in their 2015 *Harvard Business Review* article, Leaders as Decision Architects, made a neat summary of some of the more common cognitive biases that occur in a business context. How many of these have you seen?

Biases Related to Perceiving and Judging Alternatives

- CONFIRMATION BIAS: We place extra value on evidence consistent with a favoured belief and not enough on evidence that contradicts it. We fail to search impartially for evidence.
- ANCHORING AND INSUFFICIENT ADJUSTMENT: We anchor our decisions in an initial value and fail to sufficiently adjust our thinking away from that value.
- EGOCENTRISM: We focus too narrowly on our own perspective to the point that we can't imagine how others will be affected by a policy or strategy. We assume that everyone has access to the same information we do.

Biases Related to the Framing of Alternatives

- LOSS AVERSION: We feel losses more acutely than gains of the same amount, which makes us more risk-averse than a rational calculation would recommend.
- SUNK-COST FALLACY: We pay attention to historical costs that are not recoverable when considering future courses of action.
- ESCALATION OF COMMITMENT: We invest additional resources in an apparently losing proposition because of the effort, money, and time already invested.
- CONTROLLABILITY BIAS: We believe we can control outcomes more than is actually the case, causing us to misjudge the riskiness of a course of action.

Action-Oriented Biases

- EXCESSIVE OPTIMISM: We are overly optimistic about the outcome of planned actions. We overestimate the likelihood of positive events and underestimate that of negative ones.
- OVERCONFIDENCE: We overestimate our skill level relative to others' and consequently our ability to affect future outcomes. We take credit for past positive outcomes without acknowledging the role of chance.

Stability Biases

- STATUS QUO BIAS: We prefer the status quo in the absence of pressure to change it.
- PRESENT BIAS: We value immediate rewards very highly and undervalue long-term gains

Anchoring is one of the oldest sales tricks. We have all experienced the situation where a salesperson offers a product at an inflated price and then offers an alternative product at a lower price thus making it look like a bargain!
Politicians use loss aversion by spending more time working on our fears than our dreams.
Confirmation bias, egocentrism, sunk-cost fallacy, and escalation of commitment combine to explain why some companies fail to move away from a failing business model.
Status quo bias explains why we don't look for alternative quotes when we receive our car insurance renewal notification. To counter status quo bias, ask *"If the status quo were not the status quo would I choose it ahead of all the possible options?"*
Overcoming biases is easier said than done. Like it or not, we all have biases. Including you. At one of AIM WA's Professional Development Sundowner presentations, Dr Shaun Ridley FAIM said, "If you have a brain you have biases." The key to overcoming biases is to develop awareness of one's biases and to listen to others' points of view, especially contrary perspectives.

> *"If you have a brain you have biases."*
>
> *Dr Shaun Ridley FAIM*

> *"It is easy to see the faults of others, but difficult to see one's own faults. One shows the faults of others like chaff winnowed in the wind, but one conceals one's own faults as a cunning gambler conceals his dice."*
>
> *Buddha*

Self-awareness and seeking feedback from others are the best antidotes to the negative effects of cognitive biases. Therefore, one would think, a cohesive team would be immune from cognitive biases. Not so!

Enter Groupthink.

Groupthink is a cognitive bias that can apply to U (the team) and U (the business). When Groupthink pops up in the recipe, the intelligence of the group becomes much lower than the average intelligence of the group members. The result is the group members think alike and follow the same illusions. Groupthink is like a rotten ingredient that spoils the whole recipe. It is the ingredient that has flopped some of the world's biggest organizations.

In 2004, in the *Journal of Management Development*, Geoff Sheard and Andrew Kakabadse identified eight characteristics of Groupthink:

- Little or no debate about issues.
- Little or no challenging of a decision once made.
- Little or no self-criticism.
- Lots of self-congratulation.
- Defensiveness against criticism or challenge.
- A sense of "us against the world".
- An absolute conviction that the team is right.
- Declining interest in facts or opinions from outside the team.

How many of these characteristics do you recognise in your team or business? How many of these characteristics do you recognise in other teams or businesses? Is it easier to see the faults of others?

Be aware of Groupthink. Recognise its characteristics. Before it spoils your recipe.

A well-balanced team, that thinks diversely, as opposed to being cosmetically diverse, has the best chance of countering biases. Teams that boast of being "like minded" are most likely to suffer from Groupthink. People who think alike are likely to follow the same illusions.

Profiling tools such as Belbin® Team Roles, DiSC®, PRINT ® and LMAP are valuable in assembling a truly diverse and balanced team. It is essential for team members to share profile information. Otherwise, the team becomes a team of fault-concealing gamblers!

The 2020 World Economic Forum (WEF) Annual General Meeting was held in Davos-Klosters, Switzerland from 20 to

24 January 2020. The WEF's website described the meeting as the bringing together of "the world's top academics, politicians, business, and civil society leaders to engage in addressing the most pressing issues on the global agenda". The meeting had 823 public speakers with 'expert knowledge' across 7 themes of 'diverse content'. The themes were Beyond Geopolitics, Society & Future of Works, Tech for Good, Fairer Economies, Healthy Futures, Better Business, and How to Save the Planet.

COVID-19 was not on the agenda. Understandably, because COVID-19 was, at the time, in its infancy (the first case was reported in Wuhan, China in December 2019). Nevertheless, to the credit of the organizers, on 23 January 2020, COVID-19 was highlighted at the Davos Issue Briefing Room in a perceptive, accurate, and inciteful panel discussion. The significance of the COVID-19 threat and measures to defend against the virus were also highlighted in Borge Brende's Closing Remarks: The Road Ahead.

However, many post Davos publications such as *Davos 2020: What mattered*, *What We Learned At The World Economic Forum: Key Takeaways From Global Leaders*; *2020 World Economic Forum: 6 takeaways from Davos*; and *Key Take Aways From Davos 2020*, made no mention of what became a global pandemic. The explanation lies in Groupthink. Quite simply, because COVID-19 was not on the published agenda, selective focus on established issues and priorities made the writers of these publications blind to the significance of the facts that were presented around COVID-19.

Our inclination to embrace sources that confirm our beliefs (confirmation bias) is further amplified by artificial intelligence algorithms that feed us more of the same, based on our internet search history. We are being continually fed confirming evidence, which reinforces our biases.

Do you have a preferred news channel that you read, watch, or listen to most of the time? If so, you are not receiving a sufficiently balanced perspective. Make the effort to gather news and information from multiple sources, including those that may make you feel slightly uncomfortable.

> *"And here we have the real poison of the social media age: there is a refusal to entertain an alternative point of view; there is a desire to embrace only those sources which confirm your own 'worldview' or 'groupthink'; in short, it's 'biased' if it challenges your own bias. It's unhealthy and profoundly damaging."*
>
> Huw Edwards

Part 3 Takeaways

'And' recognises that each ingredient plays its part. 'And' binds the ingredients together.

U is for your unique ingredients. Be the chef, not the cook!

Treble U is about you, the individual. And you, your team. And you, your business. All three levels of you are important. The purpose of an organization, the purpose of each team and the purpose of each individual are not (and need not be) the same.

It starts with you. Clarify purpose. Get Fit for Purpose. And if you're a leader, grant autonomy. If not you, who?

But it's not all about you. It's about the people you serve and how you will add value to them. Seeing things from another person's perspective is essential in working out how you will add value to the people you serve.

Be aware you have blind spots. It starts with you. The best defense against cognitive biases is heeding feedback from others. Listen. It's not all about you.

Learn to recognise the unpleasant smell of Groupthink. Before it spoils your recipe. Entertain alternative points of view. It's not all about you.

Next, we put the recipe into action.

Reader Notes:

PART 4: The recipe in action

Simple as PQRST And U is easy to recall. Maybe not as easy as ABC but easy nevertheless!

P is for Purpose and Q is for the Question: *Why do you do what you do and how will you add value to the people you serve?* The answer to the Question provides Clarity of Purpose.

Getting Fit for Purpose comes from the RST ingredients. It's not R or S or T. It's R And S And T, all aligning with your Clarity of Purpose. 'And' binds the ingredients together. U is for your Unique ingredients. U is for you, the individual. And for your team. And for your organization. U and U and U. Remember it starts with you, but it's not all about you.

Simple as PQRST And U is versatile. The recipe applies to any organization, team or individual. It can also be applied to major projects or individual tasks.

Simple as PQRST And U is simple to use, although not necessarily easy to do. But, with practice, it will become easier.

Each ingredient of *Simple as PQRST And U* plays a part in the recipe. The importance and the quantity of each ingredient depends on you and your purpose. You may have a few special ingredients of your own you would like to add. You, your team, and your organization are unique. Customise your *Simple as PQRST And U* recipe to achieve your purpose.

When applying *Simple as PQRST And U*, you will certainly find gaps between where you would like to be (the ideal) and where you are (the reality). The gaps are opportunities to increase your value. The extent of the gap and the importance of the ingredient in fulfilling your purpose provides clarity on where you should focus your efforts to add value. In the meantime, like a great chef, improvise and be creative with the ingredients you have. *Simple as PQRST And U!*

It's time to select one of your chef hats.

Be the chef

Which hat did you select? Did you select the hat of you, the individual, or the hat of your team, or the hat of your business? Remember, the purpose of your organization, the purpose of each of your teams, and your individual purpose are not (and need not be) the same. Decide on which hat you will be wearing and keep that hat on while working through your recipe. When you've finished the recipe, you can change hats.

With your selected hat firmly in place, begin with Clarity of Purpose. Like any good chef, be clear on what you're aiming to produce. Start by finding the answer to the Question: *Why do you do what you do and how will you add value to the people you serve?* The question is simple, but the answer is not necessarily easy. Don't wait for perfection. Decide. Act.

Next, add the Fit for Purpose ingredients. Some ingredients are more important than others in achieving your purpose. You may have more than enough of some ingredients, and you may not have other ingredients.

If you were baking a cake and you had an important ingredient, what would you do with it? In a moment of writer's block, I was searching for a simple answer to that question. So, I asked my wife, Colleen. Looking somewhat bemused she said, "Use it!".

And if you do not have an important ingredient, what would you do? Go out and get it!

And if you have a lot of an ingredient that is not particularly important, then swap it for ingredients you need, but don't have.

And if you don't have an ingredient that is not important, then there is no use spending time getting it. You can leave it out.

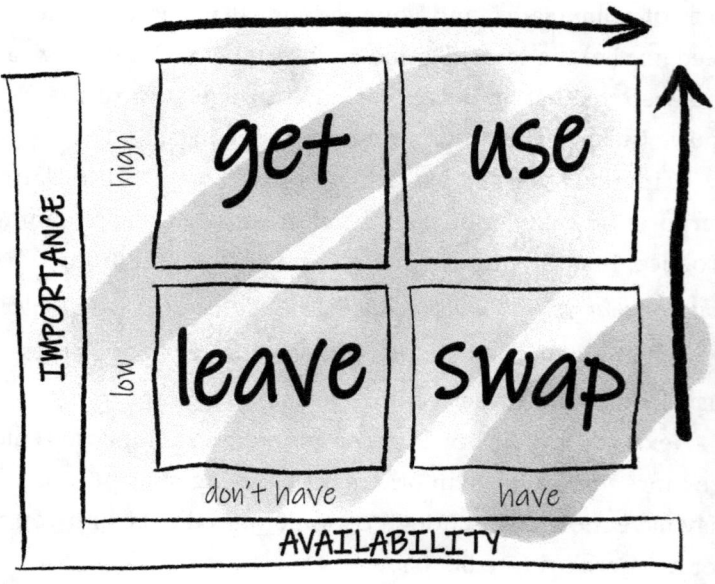

Now is the time for you to be the chef and not just a cook. Make decisions. Take action. Add value. ***Simple as PQRST And U!***

Simply sweet

Your **Simple as PQRST And U** recipe fits on a page. Elegant simplicity. **Simple as PQRST And U!**

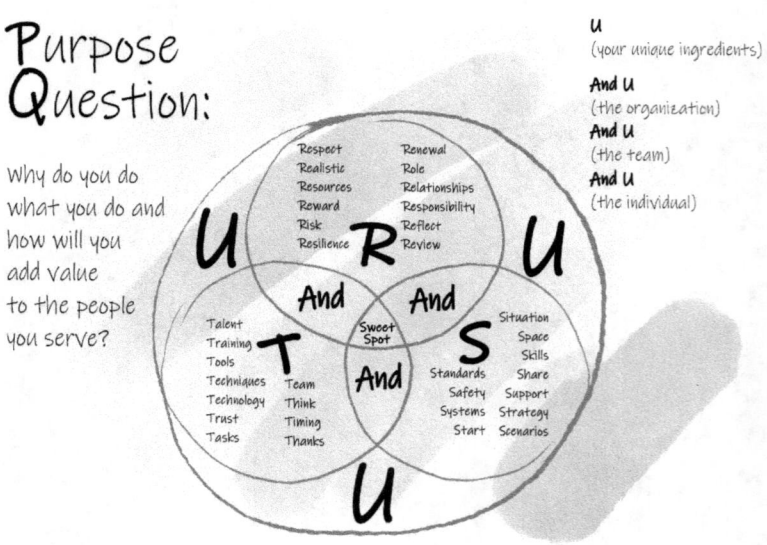

At the center of your recipe is the sweet spot, where all ingredients combine perfectly. As you refine your recipe you will expand the sweet spot, increase value, and taste the success of fulfilling your purpose.

Now let's put the recipe to the test.

The test of the recipe

My great friend and running buddy, Gordon Miles, is a psychologist in the Oncology Unit at the Perth Children's Hospital. He also has a private practice. Gordon says that running a marathon is a metaphor for life. Having run many marathons and ultra-marathons with Gordon, I identify with his analogy. **Simple as PQRST And U** applies to any task, including running a marathon. Which takes us back to Eliud Kipchoge's sub two-hour marathon.

Think about Kipchoge's Clarity of Purpose. *"To inspire many people...to tell people no human is limited"* is not about him. It's about adding value to humanity.

Think about his Fit for Purpose ingredients.

He has Resilience. He had tried two years before and failed. But that did not deter him. He Reflected and Reviewed.

He has Respect. He acknowledges the Team around him.

He uses his incredible Talent and has refined his Technique for optimal efficiency. Yet he understands that Training is essential.

He Shared his Purpose. And asked for Support. And he was supported in return.

He understood the Situation and appreciated that it would not be easy. Yet he believed he could do it.

He had a Strategy, which required efficient and sustainable use of his Resources. Timing had to be perfect. For each of the 42.2 kilometers, apart from the final kilometer, his pace varied by no more than two seconds per kilometer. Too quick too soon would mean he would run out of energy before the line. Too slow would mean he would run out of time. It wouldn't have happened if he did not Start! And, no doubt, he added his own unique ingredients.

Having planned to run ten seconds under the two-hour barrier, in the final kilometer, Kipchoge started to smile and signaled to his world class pacers to move aside. That smile said, "I've got this". Driven by his Clarity of Purpose he picked up the already blistering pace. Supported by the cheering crowds and his pacers, who were punching the air in a wave of joy behind him, Kipchoge smashed 20 seconds off the psychological two-hour barrier. He achieved more than anyone, other than perhaps himself, had thought possible.

The true test of the recipe is in the taste. Eliud Kipchoge maximized his sweet spot and tasted success. **Simple as PQRST And U!**

And so, it's time for you. U and U and U.

If not you, who? If not now, when?

It starts with you. But it's not all about you.

Your value is the sum of the decisions you make and the actions you take.

Make decisions. Take action. Add value.

It's your recipe.

Simple as PQRST And U!

Reader Notes:

Next...

Consistent with S for Support, I'm asking for your Support to contribute to the next edition of, or sequel to, **Simple as PQRST And U**. I'm asking you to Share your anecdotes and your unique ingredients. And I'm also keen to listen to your comments and suggestions. Please send them to:
 share@pqrstandu.com
 Or go to www.pqrstandu.com

You may be quoted in the next edition or sequel!

Master Chefs

This bibliography recognises the people whose ideas and concepts have added flavour to **Simple as PQRST And U**.

Beshears, J, & Gino, F 2015, 'Leaders as Decision Architects. (cover story)', *Harvard Business Review*, 93, 5, pp. 51-62.

Blenko, M. W., Mankins, M. C. and Rogers, P. (2010) 'The Decision-Driven Organization. (cover story)', *Harvard Business Review*, 88(6), pp. 54–62.

Blount, S & Leinwand, P 2019, 'Why Are We Here?', *Harvard Business Review*, vol. 97, no. 6, pp. 132–139.

Cialdini, RB 2009, *Influence: Science and practice*, 5th ed., Pearson Education, Inc., Boston.

Cialdini, RB 2001, 'Harnessing the Science of Persuasion. (cover story)', *Harvard Business Review*, vol. 79, no. 9, pp. 72–79.

Collins, J 2001, *Good to great*, Random House, London.

Covey, S 1999, *The 7 habits of highly effective people*, Simon & Schuster UK Ltd, London.

de Bono, E 1995, *Mind power*, Dorling Kindersley Limited, London.

Kahneman, D 2012, *Thinking, fast and slow*, Penguin Group (Australia), Melbourne.

Keeley, L, Pikkel, R, Quinn, B, & Walters, H 2013, *Ten types of innovation: The discipline of building breakthroughs*, John Wiley & Sons, Inc. Hoboken, New Jersey.

Peters, T 2018, *The excellence dividend*, Vintage Books, New York.

Pink, D 2018, *When: the scientific secrets of perfect timing*, Riverhead Books, New York.

Perera, G 2019, *Disruption by design*, First Step Publishing, Leederville, Australia.

Sinek, S How great leaders inspire action, TED, https://www.youtube.com/watch?v=qp0HIF3SfI4

Sinek, S 2019, *Start with Why*, Penguin Random House UK.

Sheard, AG & Kakabadse, AP 2004, 'A process perspective on leadership and team development', *Journal of Management Development*, vol. 23, no. 1, pp. 7–106.

My Unique Ingredients

Simple as PQRST And U would not have been possible without my family:

Colleen – for being my special ingredient

Hannah – "Be the pilot of your dreams"

Nicola – "This stage is too small for me. I was born to be on the big stage!"

Mom and Dad – for making me part of your recipe

My brother and sister - Garth and Kathy - for your support and feedback

Notes on Quotes

The eclectic mix of quotes in **Simple as PQRST And U** add spice to the recipe. Notes on Quotes acknowledges the people quoted and the sources of the quotes. In some cases a brief note has been added to provide further context to the quotes.

Introduction

"It's easy to take something simple and make it complex: politicians and lawyers seem to do it for a living. Yet very few innovations are championed for their intricacy. Most are known for bringing elegance and simplicity to even the thorniest problems"

Larry Keeley

Keeley, L, Pikkel, R, Quinn, B, & Walters, H 2013, *Ten types of innovation: The discipline of building breakthroughs*, John Wiley & Sons, Inc. Hoboken, New Jersey, p. 7.

Clarity of Purpose

"There are two main causes of poor decision making: insufficient motivation and cognitive biases."

John Beshears and Francesca Gino

Beshears, J, & Gino, F 2015, 'Leaders as Decision Architects. (cover story)', *Harvard Business Review*, 93, 5, p. 54.

"Purpose is the key to motivation—and motivated employees are the key to realizing your purpose. Get this symbiotic relationship right, and your organization will thrive."

Sally Blount and Paul Leinwand

Blount, S & Leinwand, P 2019, 'Why Are We Here?', Harvard Business Review, vol. 97, no. 6, pp. 132–139.

Purpose

"The purpose of a company is to engage all its stakeholders in shared and sustained value creation. In creating such value, a company serves not only its shareholders, but all its stakeholders – employees, customers, suppliers, local communities and society at large. The best way to understand and harmonize the divergent interests of all stakeholders is through a shared commitment to policies and decisions that strengthen the long-term prosperity of a company."

Klaus Schwab, Founder and Executive Chairman, World Economic Forum

https://www.weforum.org/agenda/2019/12/davos-manifesto-2020-the-universal-purpose-of-a-company-in-the-fourth-industrial-revolution/

Value

"Strive not to be a success, but rather to be of value."

Albert Einstein

https://www.brainyquote.com/quotes/albert_einstein_122232

Serve

"If I believe that as a leader, my people should be serving me, then I'm not going to be able to serve them."
John C. Maxwell
https://www.facebook.com/JohnCMaxwell/posts/if-i-believe-that-as-a-leader-my-people-should-be-serving-me-then-im-not-going-t/10157159915717954/

"Life's most persistent and urgent question is, 'What are you doing for others?'"
Martin Luther King Jr.
https://www.brainyquote.com/quotes/martin_luther_king_jr_137105

Part 1 Takeaways

"Begin with the end in mind" is Stephen R. Covey's Habit 2
Covey, S 1999, *The 7 habits of highly effective people*, Simon & Schuster UK Ltd, London.
pp. 95-144.

Realistic

Being a realistic optimist.
Heidi Grant Halvorson
Halvorson, H 2011, *Nine things successful people do differently*, Harvard Business Review Press

Reward

"Recognition is a fundamental human need. At the most basic level, it makes us feel valued, which is what inspires us to stay all bright-eyed and bushy-tailed at work. Out of all the things that matter in the workplace, helping employees feel appreciated is the most important one."

Vartika Kashyap

https://www.linkedin.com/pulse/look-around-recognise-celebrate-job-well-done-vartika-kashyap/

"Value is not determined by those who set the price. Value is determined by those who choose to pay it."

Simon Sinek

https://www.goodreads.com/quotes/886928-value-is-not-determined-by-those-who-set-the-price

Risk

"Even today, 71 percent of our members consistently say that boards are 'risk averse', and this has clear and significant implications for our capacity to respond to changing technologies and a dynamic political economy."

Angus Armour FAICD

Armour, A 2020, 'Great expectations', *Company Director*, vol. 35, 11, p. 11.

"True strategy is about placing bets and making hard choices. The objective of strategy is not to minimise risk but to increase the chance of success."

Roger Martin

Martin, RL 2014, 'The Big Lie of Strategic Planning', *Harvard Business Review*, vol. 92, no. 1/2, p. 80.

Renewal

"The self-renewal process must include balanced renewal in all four dimensions of our nature: the physical, the spiritual, the mental, and the social/emotional."

Covey, S 1999, *The 7 habits of highly effective people*, Simon & Schuster UK Ltd, London, p. 301.

Role

Serial Entrepreneur Alan Nelson anecdote from his presentation to the Wanneroo Business Association, 20 March 2019.

Reflect

"It is by three methods we may learn wisdom: First, by reflection, which is noblest; second, by imitation, which is easiest; and third by experience, which is the bitterest."

Confucius

https://www.brainyquote.com/quotes/confucius_131984

"Life is both beautiful and messy and this is your learning opportunity and your path."

Lisa McCarthy FAIM

My MBA colleague and friend Lisa McCarthy's contribution at AIM WA's book club review of Richard Reed's book *If I could tell you just one thing*.

"Life can only be understood backwards; but it must be lived forwards."

Søren Kierkegaard

https://www.brainyquote.com/quotes/soren_kierkegaard_105030

Review

"...map the future customer's journey, because you can then identify how to serve future customers and their needs."

Gihan Perera

Perera, G 2019, Disruption by design, First Step Publishing, Leederville, Australia, p. 42.

I have attended several of Gihan Perera's *Fit for the future* presentations in Perth. The story about Albert Einstein comes from one of his presentations.

"Yes, change is the basic law of nature. But the changes wrought by the passage of time affects individuals and institutions in different ways. According to Darwin's Origin of Species, **it is not the most intellectual of the species that survives; it is not the strongest that**

survives; but the species that survives is the one that is able best to adapt and adjust to the changing environment in which it finds itself. Applying this theoretical concept to us as individuals, we can state that the civilization that is able to survive is the one that is able to adapt to the changing physical, social, political, moral, and spiritual environment in which it finds itself."

Leon C. Megginson

"...in 1963 Leon C. Megginson delivered a speech that contained a passage presenting his interpretation of Charles Darwin's ideas. Megginson did not claim that he was quoting the words of Darwin. Nevertheless, over time, in a multistep process this passage has been simplified, shortened, altered, and reassigned directly to Darwin."

https://quoteinvestigator.com/2014/05/04/adapt/

Situation

"Being always in favor of or always against a particular idea makes you blind to information that doesn't fit your perspective. This is usually a bad approach if you would like to understand reality."

Rosling, H, Rosling, O, & Rosling Ronnland, A 2018, *Factfulness*, Holder & Stoughton, London, p. 186.

"A decision without the pressure of consequence is hardly a decision at all."

Eric Langmuir

https://allauthor.com/quotes/author/eric-langmuir/

Share

"We are human because our ancestors learned to share their food and their skills in an honored network of obligation"

Ascribed to Anthropologist Richard Leakey by Robert Cialdini.

Cialdini, R 2009, *Influence: Science and practice*, 5th edition, Pearson Education, Inc., Boston, p. 19.

"Doing business without advertising is like winking at a girl in the dark. You know what you're doing but nobody else does!"

Steuart Henderson Britt

https://www.goodreads.com/quotes/220047-doing-business-without-advertising-is-like-winking-at-a-girl

Strategy

"The role of the CEO is first and foremost to validate the link between a company's strategy and its purpose."

Jean-Dominique Senard, Chair, Renault

http://bit.ly/2S9O53x

Start

"Act or be acted upon"

Stephen R. Covey

Covey, S 1999, *The 7 habits of highly effective people*, Simon & Schuster UK Ltd, London, p. 76.

Jim Collins Flywheel

Collins, J 2001, *Good to great*, Random House, London, pp. 164-165.

Technology

"Data is the new natural resource, so you need to think, 'now that I've aggregated that, how do I get something useful out of it?'"

Doug Robinson, Managing Partner for IBM Services at IBM https://www.theaustralian.com.au/business/technology/how-to-build-a-selfthinking-enterprise/news-story/d8d914ecf945e7083c9788323435f638

"Problems inspire us to push the world forward. IBM is changing the way the world works by applying smart technologies at scale, with purpose and expertise. Smart loves problems. Let's put smart to work.®"

https://www.theaustralian.com.au/business/technology/how-to-build-a-selfthinking-enterprise/news-story/d8d914ecf945e7083c9788323435f638

Natalie Nguyen views on AI are from Stuart Ridley's article in the October 2019 Company Director magazine

"It is just another tool. A very powerful tool, but still a tool. You need people to make decisions."

Natalie Nguyen

Ridley, S 2019, 'The founder: Thinking in hyperdrive', Company Director, vol. 35, 09, pp. 80-81.

Team

"A team is not a bunch of people with job titles, but a congregation of individuals, each of whom has a role which is understood by other members."

Belbin® website: https://www.belbin.com/about/belbin-team-roles/

Timing

"I used to believe that timing was everything. Now I believe that everything is timing."

Daniel H. Pink

Pink, D 2018, When: the scientific secrets of perfect timing, Riverhead Books, New York, p. 218.

Treble U

"No matter one's level, industry or career, we all need to find a personal sense of meaning in what we do."

Kristi Hedges (5 Questions to Help Your Employees Find Their Inner Purpose): https://hbr.org/2017/08/5-questions-to-help-your-employees-find-their-inner-purpose

It starts with U

"The new smart will be about trying to overcome the two big inhibitors of critical thinking and team collaboration: our ego and our fears. Doing so will make it easier to perceive reality as it is, rather than as we wish it to be."

Ed Hess

'In the AI Age, "Being Smart" Will Mean Something Completely Different', *Harvard Business Review* June 2017, https://hbr.org/2017/06/in-the-ai-age-being-smart-will-mean-something-completely-different

In McKinsey's January 2020 McKinsey Classics, we are reminded of the foresight of Martin Dewshusrt and Paul Willmot in their September 2014 McKinsey Quarterly article:

"In a world where artificial intelligence supports all manner of day-to-day management decisions, the need to "let go" will be more significant and the discomfort for senior leaders higher."

Martin Dewhurst and Paul Willmott

'Manager and machine: The new leadership equation', *McKinsey Quarterly* September 2014,

https://www.mckinsey.com/featured-insights/leadership/manager-and-machine

"As AI grows in power, the likelihood of sinking under the weight of even quite valuable insights grows as well. The solution would be to democratize information by encouraging business units and functions to make more and better decisions themselves."

'How artificial intelligence changes the executive's role', *McKinsey Classics* January 2020

https://www.mckinsey.com/~/media/McKinsey/Email/Classics/2020/2020-01-classic.html

"Our reflex to protect our egos never leaves us, but as we ask ourselves different questions, we can discover—and follow—a development path that enriches us as human beings and ultimately benefits our teams, organizations, and even the world."

Jennifer Garvey Berger and Zafer Gedeon Achi

'Understanding the leader's 'identity mindtrap': Personal growth for the C-suite', *McKinsey Quarterly* January 2020,
https://www.mckinsey.com/business-functions/organization/our-insights/understanding-the-leaders-identity-mindtrap-personal-growth-for-the-c-suite

It's not all about U

"Dependent people need others to get what they want. Independent people can get what they want through their own effort. Interdependent people combine their own efforts with the efforts of others to achieve great success."

Covey, S 1999, *The 7 habits of highly effective people*, Simon & Schuster UK Ltd, London, p. 49.

"We've found that even though most people believe they are self-aware, self-awareness is a truly rare quality: We estimate that only 10%–15% of the people we studied actually fit the criteria."

"...leaders must actively work on both seeing themselves clearly and getting feedback to understand how others see them."

Dr Tasha Eurich
What Self-Awareness Really Is (and How to Cultivate It)
https://hbr.org/2018/01/what-self-awareness-really-is-and-how-to-cultivate-it

"If you know yourself and you also know others, you will not be endangered in a hundred battles"

Sun Wu (The Art of War) cited by Sun Tzu II & Cleary 1996, p. 26 in 'The lost art of war'.

"Listening isn't just hearing; it requires the willingness to entertain other viewpoints—especially opposing ones."
Ram Charan interview with Melinda Merino 2013
You Can't Be a Wimp—Make the Tough Calls
https://hbr.org/2013/11/you-cant-be-a-wimp-make-the-tough-calls

Blind U

Daniel Kahneman refers to The Invisible Gorilla study by Christopher Chabris and Daniel Simons.
The video is available here: https://www.youtube.com/watch?v=vJG698U2Mvo
"The gorilla study illustrates the two important facts about our minds: we can be blind to the obvious, and we are also blind to our blindness."
Kahneman, D 2012, *Thinking, fast and slow*, Penguin Group (Australia), Melbourne, p. 24

"It is easy to see the faults of others, but difficult to see one's own faults. One shows the faults of others like chaff winnowed in the wind, but one conceals one's own faults as a cunning gambler conceals his dice."
Buddha
https://fakebuddhaquotes.com/real-buddha-quotes/

Cognitive biases
Beshears, J, & Gino, F 2015, 'Leaders as Decision Architects. (cover story)', *Harvard Business Review*, 93, 5, pp. 51-62.

Characteristics of Groupthink

Sheard, AG & Kakabadse, AP 2004, 'A process perspective on leadership and team development', *Journal of Management Development*, vol. 23, no. 1, p. 14.

Davos 2020 agenda

https://www.weforum.org/agenda/2020/01/health-healthcare-davos2020/

Davos 2020 Issue Briefing Room

https://www.weforum.org/events/world-economic-forum-annual-meeting-2020/sessions/update-wuhan-coronavirus

Davos 2020 Borge Brende's Closing Remarks: The Road Ahead

https://www.weforum.org/events/world-economic-forum-annual-meeting-2020/sessions/closing-remarks-the-road-ahead-48ec1e3eea

"And here we have the real poison of the social media age: there is a refusal to entertain an alternative point of view; there is a desire to embrace only those sources which confirm your own 'worldview' or 'groupthink'; in short, it's 'biased' if it challenges your own bias. It's unhealthy and profoundly damaging."

Huw Edwards, Chief Anchor, BBC News at Ten, https://www.linkedin.com/pulse/ge19-from-presenters-chair-huw-edwards/

About the Author

Randal Wells is the Founder and Managing Director of Welldev Group Pty Ltd (Welldev). His personal mantra, and that of Welldev is: *Your value is the sum of the decisions you make and the actions you take.*

Randal is a Fellow of the Australian Institute of Management WA (AIMWA), a Graduate of the Australian Institute of Company Directors (GAICD) and an alumnus of Leadership WA. In 2017 Randal became AIMWA's inaugural MBA graduate. He volunteers as a mentor with AIMWA's mentor/mentee program.

Randal lives in Perth, Western Australia with his wife, Colleen, and daughters Hannah and Nicola. He grew up in Kwa-Zulu Natal, South Africa and was high schooled at Michaelhouse. He attended Natal University where he graduated with a Bachelor of Science in Civil Engineering, and then completed two years' military national service with the South African Defense Force where he became a Lieutenant in the Corps of Engineers. He then commenced his working career and became a professionally registered (PrEng) civil engineer. During this time, he studied part-time at the University of South Africa and graduated with a Bachelor of Commerce Honours degree, which led to him towards a career change to business and property development.

Sport plays an important part in Randal's life. He is a sub three-hour marathon runner and has silver medals for both the Comrades and Two Oceans ultra-marathons. He views running as the purest of sports because success does not depend on having expensive equipment or facilities. Randal also enjoys playing social golf and cricket. It is no coincidence that sporting anecdotes find their way into ***Simple as PQRST And U***.

www.ingramcontent.com/pod-product-compliance
Lightning Source LLC
Chambersburg PA
CBHW070308010526
44107CB00056B/2530